A COLLECTION OF GROWING UP POEMS

Odey Richard Odey

CONTENTS

PREFACE

Once upon a time, in the enchanted land of my childhood, there lived a wild imagination bursting to be set free. As I grew into my teenage years, life decided to play a game of rollercoaster with me. But fear not, for I discovered a magical secret to surviving the twists and turns—I wielded the mighty power of the written word!

Ah, the joys of being a closet introvert! With no one to confide in or share my deepest thoughts with, I found solace in a trusty companion: my trusty pencil and a blank sheet of paper. And when the paper was nowhere to be found, fear not, dear friends, for I hatched poems in the depths of my mind, nurturing them until they could be freed from their cerebral prison.

Oh, the therapy of it all! This simple act of releasing the musings of my mind became a lifeline, a flotation device in the tempestuous sea of life. The issues that threatened to detonate within me found an escape route through the ink of my pen. Those poems, my dear friends, were my personal treasure trove.

But wait, the adventure doesn't end there! This growing collection of poems accompanied me through every twist and turn. From the hallowed halls of the university to the heart-pounding trials of army life, even during lengthy peacekeeping operations and my constant travels within Nigeria and beyond.

Alas, technology had a wicked sense of humor. My first computer played a cruel trick, crashing and devouring my precious poems. Panic ensued, tears were shed, but fear not, for I emerged as a warrior, rewriting them by hand and typing them once more. But oh, the fates laughed heartily and sent another crash to challenge my resolve. The cycle repeated, a dance with fate that could rival the best African dance to frenzied tomtoms.

And so, in a moment of epiphany, a thought blossomed like a vegetable patch in a desert: What if I lost them forever? Why hide these poems away? I was but a humble custodian of the words, an architect of emotions, and they deserved to see the light of day. Like a reckless daredevil, I took a leap of faith and published them, unadorned and true.

Dear readers, my cherished poems still remain a feast for my soul. But perhaps, just perhaps, they might find their way into your hearts too. Perhaps you, like a kindred spirit, have danced with similar experiences. And if you haven't, fear not, for I invite you on a whimsical journey through the trials and tribulations of an African boy and his quest to conquer the whims of growing up.

So buckle up, my dear friends, as we embark on this adventure together. Let the poems weave their magic and transport you to a world where laughter, tears, and a touch of mischief await. Let's uncover the wonders of life, one verse at a time.

A HARVEST OF FIGMENTS

What undisclosable secrets lurk in your breast?

What insatiable desires fire you ceaselessly

That you seek to substantiate the abstract,

Make thoughts and emotions palpable?

What do you so much yearn to reveal

In its absolute form and wholeness

On paper, paint, wood and stone,

In clay, horn, iron and bone?

You know no axewoman lodges in the moon,

No Orion ever spanned the skies,

No leviathan rocks the marine waves,

And no Neptune dwells deep beneath.

Yet you labor at that elusive idea,

A little bit in the morning light,

And the last thing at night,

But it remains just out of reach.

And you know no Atlas holds up the world,

No Vulcan stokes a subterranean furnace;

If it isn't all lies,

Let the god of fire dare show his blackened face.

Note: A Harvest of Figments is about the struggle of an artist, or a writer, to express their identity. They put themselves in a position where it might be said to them, "You're building castles in the air!" Sometimes it is easy to forget that there never was a castle that was not first built in the "air" of the imagination.

MY STAND

I draw my calm, like the harried wind vane,

From raging storms, plundering winds and pain.

The night poultices my hara-kiri,

Its cool, dark tonic cauterizing me.

I fall to glory, lose to success,

At last, I sing a dirge; death, please dance.

Note: I invented a personal brand of stoic philosophy to help me withstand the rigors of life in the army, and even outside it. The philosophy consists of observing an army axiom that urges you to "zero your mind". This zeroing of the mind is the greatest piece of truism invented by the Nigerian army for the professional survivalist that each soldier should be. It means for you to assume total invulnerability even in the face of the greatest odds whenever there is a job that has to be done. It might sound fatalistic, and even senseless, but it works, especially when one has no other option; it is the stuff that brings victory over enemies, no matter their advantages. It is the stuff of battlefield magic. During problems that could mean disaster for many, I tried to weather the storm and survive by looking for the calm eye in the center of the hurricane.

AFUFU; THE WIND

I am Afufu,

The caster down upon mighty crown

Even the mighty Imocha,

Uprooting buttress-skirts,

That vitals secreted deeply in the earth

Might be revealed, naked,

To the patient, grinning sun.

I caress, I buffet,

And sometimes I pack an hour's fondling

Into a single second.

Upon my breakers

I plant my feet and bounce

Trailing verdure or rubble,

Vitality or corpses.

I, the maker,

The sustainer

And the slayer,

Wield transparent weight

In my only-felt palms.

Unleashed,

There is no sanctuary enough from me.

Alone,

I knit with the silent cosmos,

Wherever I alight on being,

There are singing and dancing,

And I am.

Note: Afufu means the breeze in my language. The breeze can be a destructive storm, an indifferent wind or a life-giving zephyr. I'm fascinated by the awesome contradictory powers of the air in its various personas. It is personified by a person who does not only live to eat, sleep and multiply but also to impact the world. The *imocha* is a mighty tree in my language.

A WARNING INCANTATION

Let the owner of his head hold it

From I that cook with venom.

What is the name that we call affliction?

What is the name that we call death?

It is the man who seeks my wife...

But a mysterious death surpasses hearsay;

If the dog that eats my intestines survives,

Madness will not go by it...

If the house-rat hears,

Let him fill the bush rat's ears.

Note: This is a Yoruba incantation that I heard on TV when I was about thirteen years old. Its poetry resonated with me and I quickly penned it down in English, hoping to catch its poignancy. It is an admonition to would-be trespassers across the sacred boundary of the family.

MY SKULL

Let us be grateful to civilisation

For locking me in its straight jacket,

Preventing me from at once following

The surging of white-hot adrenaline

Raised by the storm of ordinary words

As it rushed on in eager waves

Through the mysterious constrictions of my veins

Making my trembling and sweating palms

To itch for some primordial stone weapons,

Eliciting a full-grown chest-growl

From my knotted throat and quivering nose

Sniffing out the aroma of fresh blood,

And a skull to add to my memento…

You leave the fresh head for a few slow weeks

In a termitarium's belly

That the dross may be removed

Then you extricate you gleaming trophy

To keep in a warrior's dark hiding place…

Before you march home to smash with your cutlass

Your wife's pot singing merrily on the fire,

All because of a few spoken words;

And it's because of civilization

That I cannot now claim my skull.

Note: Before colonization, tribal warriors in my village and the surrounding villages were members of a secret society. Even when there was no war to be fought, the members of the secret society had to prove their manhood by bringing home a fresh human skull gained during single combat. The warrior's status is recognised according to the number of the skulls that he has in his possession, and which are displayed during his funeral when he dies. Nowadays, the restraint placed on us as members of the human society as statehood and Law has enabled us to live in relative security from the actions of individuals infuriated by mere words, or the action of others. Sometimes when one is spurred into anger, one has only to think of long years in prison in order to advise oneself and temper one's actions, even thoughts.

INTIMATIONS OF NEW SEASONS

In my bones, in my heart,

In my brain, in my mind,

In the very core of my existence,

Grasping my trove's key in mystic palms

Upon cold haunches,

Glaring around my inner cardinal points,

Purging my soul of all but a longing,

A yearning, a craving, a devouring abysm

Gaping ravenously with passing time,

Spawned of years of unlearning,

Is that mind-sucking vampire, ignorance.

I waited one, two, three, four, five years

While I kept my bowl upturned,

Head dozing between my knees…

But I looked up after the comet

To find a startling meteorite in my bowl.

Prohibited from hurling it back, I waited

The span of the harvest of the ripest dreams,

Dead seeds and rusted hoes in my hands,

At the edge of farmland spread like outer space,

Neither digging nor planting,

Desiring harvest, dreaming possible fruits

Until the spiders of ignorance

Cocooned me in their webs.

Note: Hope comes with the approaching of a positive change in the state of affairs. The ambition of a man goes along with his vicissitude in the process of achieving it. But hope is treacherous at times; at the very moment of realization, it could disappoint. It begins to seem as if it is by chance that dreams are realized.

ANOTHER NEW SEASON

The fires rekindle once again,
The smoldering coals leap into flames,
Rousing my somnolent Muse again
From its forced earthbound slumber.

So, sing, my Muse, sing.
Never keep silent.
Never seal your lips
Keeping it all caged in my breast.

Free your sweetest tongues
To sing my song in mellifluous songs.
Should I command, cajole, deceive you,
Or lead you by a ring in your nose?

Begin to speak again
And stop staring like a dumb statue
With the speechlessness of a corpse.

What I need is for you to sing.

Do you need palm oil or pigeon blood,

Before you sing of my old vision,

Before you dip your tongue into my mind

And drink from the well of my inspiration?

Then sing of that lost Eastern evening,

The dying sun setting in me

In an aurora of engulfing flame,

Expanding until I became the flame...

Oh, sweet joy, forever do not cloy.

Remain, like an eternal rainbow

Painted forever in my being,

Leaving me beautiful forever.

Note: Every writer fights with this personal fountain of inspiration in the effort to make tangible the indefinite ideas that inhabit his mind. I lost a collection of poems, essays, and other writings that I had been working on for years when my desktop computer crashed. Then my laptop, on which I did my backup, was stolen from my technician. This brought me to a certain futility of writing, from which I had to fight my way out.

TO HUNGER

You treacherous friend,

After all these years of familiarity, after our age long togetherness,

So early this morning

You begin to claw and gnaw ceaselessly

It surprises me how in this modern world

I should suffer such an ancient ailment.

So I wear a shirt to cover my belly

That the x-ray eyes of men

May not reveal its gnawing emptiness

Sucking at my flesh, bones, brains, and spirit.

I stay indoors all day long

Practicing the yoga of self-conservation,

My stomach pressed hard into my sofa,

My elbows dug deeply into my sides.

I take occasional glasses of water

That stands between complete fasting and me.

You won't even let me

Digest these sweet verses.

After all these years of you and me

Your malice still lurks within, aestivating.

Is there no truce, no being hardened

Or getting used to you at all?

Friends of long become one,

In spirit if not in form,

But not you. Not you!

You must dissent,

Contrariness is your meat.

You hone your teeth upon it and much

Until you have seen me supine upon my stomach

From morning until the evening,

My legs wasted like an old man's,

My hands trembling no unlike his...

And my eyelids uncooperative gossamer.

It is then you spread your airy feasts

In my fitful dreams,

Transforming me into a rebellious blasphemer...

Go on! By all means, go on,

You Caliban, gnaw and eat until you are bloated,

After all, I can't deny you harbor.

But one glorious day

You shall find the wharf desert-dry.

Maybe that was your ultimate aim

And you will be laughing.

Well, I'll be laughing too.

Note: Hunger is a normal part of life in Sub-Saharan Africa. This may sound strange to westerners, but it is true. I cannot calculate how many times I have gone hungry; hunger was a constant accompaniment to me in my growing years, and even beyond. At times it was due to lack, at other times it was due to unavoidable situations. Nevertheless, hunger is hunger, and like training to withstand thirst, one will forever fail to get used to it.

ON THE DEATH OF A BUTTERFLY

Whatever tempted out a butterfly

On a night for a tiger moth

Must have sat up to weave the dubious web

That tickled them out to a destiny both.

It must have spilt to cause the very lack

That finally lit oil in a can,

In a last stand against the pressing dark,

To burn and beat it back until dawn.

It also must have lured the flirting fly

Driven from sleep out of some cozy liar

On a moth's night, to enjoy, live and die,

Enraptured with an oil-lamp fire.

And in flitted the floral fly

To flirt around the fickle flame,

To weave, to bob, weaving to the lamp's sigh

Complex tapestries of rhapsody none the same.

The coquettish basking not nearly enough

It rushed with its smothering wings its sun.

It rushed now and again to blow off

The lamp and seemed to find it much fun

Until it dived into molten butter

And cloyed its wings as if about to die,

About to die it began to flutter

A shredded beauty, a foolish flaming fly.

Note: One night, a long time ago, I watched helplessly as a butterfly, like a kamikaze pilot, repeatedly dashed into the flame of an oil lamp.

DOOMSDAY

I get mad

Then I sneak out

Of the house

Like a mouse

To the road

To withhold

My boiling offal

As I suffer

The bludgeon

Of the demon

Of my mother

And Lucifer

And the hell

Of biased gospel

Full of culture

For my torture.

I dare not speak

So I sulk

Than be called

Of oppression, and galled.

I keep shut

And steam hot

Until I can't stop;

Then I blew up.

Note: I was becoming a cynical teenager, wondering at the incongruity between the existence of an Omnipotent Benevolence and all that I considered evil. I began to think that my mother was laying it on too thickly with her religious beliefs and we often had arguments on the matter.

A HOUSE IN MEMORIAM

Stern regiments of flamboyant trees,

Moats of scrawny spider lilies,

Ancient coconut trees, prurient fingers wide,

Pensive kingfishers staring

Thoughtfully at the fishless tap puddles

Behind the house, make do

With toads and lizards

Colonizing the dead Doctor's former house.

The coconuts weep sweet tears

Before hurling their lachrymose selves to death,

When the rampaging storm reminds them of their master.

The flaming soldiers froze in their ranks,

Like immortal rattler-armed sentries

Warding off even invisible feints

From the mystery of the invading forests,

Preserving, in the decaying shadows of the leafy museum,

Preserving for the tribal-marked academic,

When his brains had been shed on the highway.

We drunked to the road

Beyond the portal of his bread,

Now the door of his beyond,

To be besotted

With the splattered inside of the head

Of he that lived by his head.

Note: I want to believe that death is traumatizing to every child. When the doctor got killed outside the main gate of the Cocoa Research Institute, people went there to see the gory sight. For many weeks after, as we crossed the same dangerous highway on our way to the primary school, I would try not to look at the dried bloodstains and brain matter that marked the tarmac where the car ran into him; I never succeeded. When my father achieved senior staff we had to move to the senior staff quarters, and our house was just a street away from the late doctor's house. Fruit trees, ornamental trees, and flowers gone wild had joined hands with wild trees and shrubs to overrun the extensive compound, and I had this impression of trespassing whenever we passed through the compound, sometimes as a shortcut, sometimes in search of crickets to roast.

ABIKU

O pitiless insatiable infernal incarnate,

Maddened by your thirst for libation,

For the blood of labor,

For the tears of birthing and mourning,

You are spurred

By your plethora of pampered desires

And surfeit satisfaction

Of your past wilful cruel sojourns

And your incessant escapes by your weird arts,

From the fetters of cowries

Charmed with banishing incantation

To come back once again to torture and desecrate

The sanctity of our motherhood.

You victim of hostile blades and knives,

Mutilated, dismembered, and burnt,

Broadcast upon unfamiliar waters

That you may for once learn your lesson,

Again you surmount mystical impregnability,

To clone, whole and unamputated,

From your very ashes and dust.

You love the damp hums so much,

But you will never stay there for long.

Unafraid of that your age long reception,

From your liar in the evil forest,

Your night-eyes, sensing fecund home,

You still grope with your coldblooded fingers

For the innocently encompassing warmth,

Another hopeful womb.

Note: This is my own take on the phenomenon of Abiku. It is a Yoruba word that means, "Born to die". The word comes from the time before modern medicine, when child mortality was a given and mothers were not sure that their child would survive. Sometimes, women have repeated stillbirths or lose their children at infancy to what is now recognised as sickle cell diseases, or some other congenital illnesses. When this happens, among the Yoruba, the dead child may be dismembered and the pieces scattered in the forest or in the river in the hope of deterring it from coming back as another fetus. I grew up in Yorubaland and such stories were staples on which we were raised and traumatized me.

ISAAC AT IBADAN

By the irreverent traffic's sunken bank

Oozing its unconcerned, unbroken way

In non traditional and modern discordance,

Barely hanging unto his third leg,

In a grandly grimy rusted ofi

Creaking in protest

Like rusty blacksmith hinges,

Stood a withered old man.

Shrunken single-seed-in-a-pod body

As dignifiedly old

As Clark's gold,

He hauled up a wasted arm

To beg once again

The stonily staring blind traffic

An inconsequential passage.

For long bitter minutes

The memories of muscled youth,

The gone ancient days
Of unbroken horses,
The lost ways of words and swords,
Iron chains and tattooed lords
Came back to him.

Weary of lowering
His conquered hand again unanswered
His quenched eyes
Clambered up his arm's parchment
To the crazy peak
And peered questioningly at his Creator.

Shivering in the impatience of age,
Long-becalmed eyes darted about,
Moldy tongue slithering, like a vermin,
Over dried and lacerated lips,
He made his unrehearsed way,
Like the first day on stilts,
Across the expressway.

Who stemmed the rushing rapids?
Who removed the thorns, shards and boulders?
Who was so bold to step on the highway codes?

A faint murmur of the tired breeze

Mumbling like the thoughtless wind

That spent itself whipping up the waves at sea

And is now too weakened to speak out,

Wafted past him,

Past my windshield, and,

Like the fragrance of some unseen blossoms,

Rubbed off from the breeze.

I perceived on the tip of my drawn senses the blessing

"May you grow old".

Note: I had just finished secondary school and had begun to venture into ancient, overcrowded Ibadan city. On one such occasion, as I was trying to cross to the other side of the road, I saw a very old man trying to cross and being driven back by the uncaring traffic. I stepped into the actually crawling traffic, stopped the flow momentarily, and escorted the man to the other side. The Yorubas believe very much in the powers of curses or prayers, so the man turned around and prayed for me.

THE SONG OF A RAM

The somnolent monarch of the night,

Waking up from a twenty-eight days slumber,

Lifted his silvery eye-brow

To observe the annual sacrifice.

A wary crust of timeless star

Waged astronomical war

Against the gleaming almost dental arc

Scrutinizing his regal domain.

The last droplets in a drying well

Is sweetest to the drink drinking throat

Yet the most loathsome to the well

For it is the dregs of life... so a horse

I became; to every urchin, I became

The victim-champion of town-wide ram-battles,

Ridden sore and fought aching...

Life withered into tediousness.

Seven days to that juncture, I was tethered

To be fed lovingly

By the very hand that flogged and stoned,

And engorged upon the erstwhile preserve

Of the Turbaned One's granary,

But now served none other than me. I munched

To the serenade of an ancient blood-melody

Wafting home from a strange, captivating melody.

On the eve, my soul sliced the chord.

I listened to it weeping

Out in the windy wasteland of life.

I heard the sound of defeated desires

Toying with the safety of my being.

Terrified, I absconded with the debt,

My unsalaamed getaway

Left discord-sowed footprints in their hearts.

"O sweet wrapping substance of night,

Conceal me in your void.

Drape your abysmal cloak over my flight…"

But their might came upon them,

Whirling my path into a tightening vortex,

A spinning top within the hounds baying nearer

Until I ceased the fight within daggered robes.

Then I was incarcerated, my dot of a life

Filling the span of my jail as I watched

The day illuminates my own last supper.

I sought to postpone the dreaded moment

When I intersect with the dreaded scythe.

Always, rejuvenating prayers

Before it was shed.

The whetted blade hovered, then descended,

Razoring through the abruptly ended,

My treacherous ears blindfolding my eyes,

My own ears. And the ram bled.

Note: It is common to slaughter animals with a sharpened knife in Africa. I had just witnessed a nearly botched slaughtering. It mixed with the tales of the same thing being done to humans that my aunty had witnessed just before the horror of the Nigerian civil war, and I wondered, "what if I was a ram?"

22, OCTOBER

What thread of fate tied the queen

To the 178 subjects in the iron bird,

That of the entire

Nine hundred and twenty-three million

Seven hundred and sixty-eight square miles

That made up the kingdom,

It should find nowhere else to plunge

Beyond the prying eyes of any committee

Into the sod of the king's land?

Could it be the handiwork of terrorists?

Or ill tutored pilots

Or the tiredness of aged engines and metal

Or an appointed intersection

With a fated thunderbolt?

All studies of free will and destiny

Cannot proceed beyond mere theory,

If we cannot unravel the mystery

But only dwell on conjecture.

If only one prescient man,

A truly seeing witchdoctor

Existed somewhere in this world,

This would have been averted;

But there was no prophecy,

No forewarning vision or dream,

No Janus-faced riddles Delphic riddles,

Just a concluded suddenness

Now securely in the unalterable past.

Note: On that date, an aircraft plunged to the ground killing all the passengers it was carrying. At that time many of the miracle churches of Nigeria were in their infancy and the fact that none of them could prophesy and therefore avert the accident effectively debunked all such claims to me.

THE LAST SAY

Through the tarry slopes of warnings,

Fearful prognosis and insulting predictions,

Like predilection, like destiny, like doom,

Scrambling, slipping, crawling, fighting,

They slithered irrevocable down to the greatest craving,

To bask in the aura of the Light.

The bedraggled shipwrecked sailor

Crept ashore onto what from the rough sea

Was a smiling arc of luxuriant beach,

Heavenly lassitude for the heavily laden

And touched the scepter,

Felt the infinitesimal jot of ebbing power--

Only a tiny electron lost from a universal whole.

Rather than the desired condescension,

The smile of the indulgent benefactor,

He splintered their heads with the hefted symbol;

The heads were proffered, all scepters metal,

That they were brained then scarcely astounds.

My much-desired,

My soul's motive,

Is no more.

Yet they are...tantalizingly close by,

Like the shimmering images of ever-shifting greener

Ever thwarting the sun-smote traveler's heart,

Ever near, yet so far away...

And I, alone, questing for soul communion

Unfolded my palm from the one lone kernel,

The last gem I now refuse to bequeath,

Proof and symbol of oneness and loneliness.

Note: I quickly realized the connection between rampant religious belief and the disordering of the mind, especially in the uneducated, superstitious and unwary classes. This has led to deaths and the ripping apart of families as Pentecostal pastors of what we know here in Nigeria as "mushroom churches" turn what should have been a beautiful worship experience into a lifetime horror for many.

FOR LIEUTENANT JOHNSON

You were mown down before the time

Like a pernicious weed in someone's garden.

Your early dusk has set the way

For famine to descend on us.

Can I ever forget those walks

In the depths of cocoa forests

With tiny me on your atlas shoulders,

My ears filled with soft symphonies.

Every time we were together

We were like the blackened white keys,

Handel's Hallelujah Chorus

Hallucinating in my head.

I think of those your gangling limbs

That strode and ran victoriously,

Will they now, in a wooden box,

Be confined to lie forever so still?

There was nothing we couldn't have done

If you hadn't suddenly gone away

While you were the awaited crop.

Now, I face the whole world alone.

Farewell, beloved kinsman,

We shall see you no more.

Let it be to your heart's desire you go,

The sea-tossed sailor shoreward borne.

Note: Lieutenant Johnson was my mother's younger brother. He was well educated, over six feet tall and a supreme athlete. He was to my boyish eyes the greatest man that ever lived, and the only hero a boy needed. I loved him so much that I wanted to be like him, but before the mold could set in, he died at the University College Hospital at Ibadan. The bereavement left such a gaping hole in our family and hearts that is yet unfilled.

FUNERAL IN YALA TOWN

No one could tell the sorrowful tears

From the spittle of watering mouths;

They so mingled on the faces of the sympathizers

Mourning the dead, and, on further thoughts,

The unfortunate incontinence of their stomachs.

After serious pondering refined by mourning,

Unanimous verdict held food and beer

As accomplices in homicide.

They ate and drank them mercilessly,

Leaving the plates and bottles justly empty.

"Then, call in the drummer. Let him sooth

Their disheveled hearts. In truth,

Sadness reigns there. Let him

Drum it out of there".

No one really meant to dance,

Only renegade feet could not resist prancing.

Their tear-soaked faces watched helplessly

As their feet skipped around heedlessly.

Note: I'm forever astonished and horrified at the funerals organized at the death of a relative in my village. It is almost as if the mourners are celebrating the demise of the deceased with money that they could not spare while the dead was alive, or even on his deathbed in a hospital.

A WARNING

The primordial urge coursing through me

Sent me of a quest

From which I never awake but in heat.

In spite of dire consequences,

Both in this life and the coming death,

Assailing the only religion

That is the mold of my conscience.

They grew on the golden symbol,

Innocuously dormant today,

Virulently pestilential tomorrow;

Love, lust, biology and religion

Roars around my brooding head

In a whirling phantasmagoria

Of fate and its possibilities

Into which I plunge my hands.

It penetrated empirically,

Through the distant echoes, the faint scents,

Dim visions of clouding of cloudy scenes wafting

Through the claddings of procrastination,

Years of microbial corrosion

Starts to eat through the battlements,

Eliciting a blinding dusk

From the opus buried within,

Through which I grope for my saga;

Mad, impotent and infertile men,

Searching for a panacea.

They throng into herbalists' shrines,

They go from ectomy to ectomy,

To radiotherapeutic furnaces,

While I remain cozily ensconced

In my cocoon of schadenfreude;

I'm invulnerable.

Note: Without guidance I found myself confused about life, having to make difficult choices and improvising along the way. I was not deluded about the future effects of my choices but at times there was nothing I could do than to shrug mentally.

COMING OF AGE

Despite my old yearning,

What I seek retreats,

And time hurries past

A harried fiend, vainly vying,

An errant breeze, urgently fleeing,

Outdoing pursuers, yet flying still faster.

They declare, "Mind not,

Not all is yet lost.

But my beardless prime

Eloped with aged Time.

So, time the Healer

Turns the Killer;

As much as it healing breathe

Is its sting of death.

Then I grow ripe,

Busting with sweet sap.

Let not my joy dampen

From the knowledge that maturing

Walks hand in hand with rotting.

Note: A favorite childhood pastime in which I spent many hours was to become a grown-up. But as I became a teenager, and adulthood approached, I began to understand that being grown up comes with a negative correlation that is bitter if not coupled with social mobility.

DRY SEASON WIT

Asphyxiating warren stifled me.

Humid and sickly, I expectorated it.

The doorway engorged, transmitted me

Into the core of without this cruel season.

All around stifling pinstriped coats and trousers

Swaddled in gasping hairless apes survived

Gaping from skyscraper windows and from there

Contemplating messy season-driven suicides.

The robber-wind rushed by with howling cars in it.

The sweltering earth dropped upwards to the sky

Seeking out the reluctant mustard-seed raindrops.

By me flew past a dismal mangy cur

Valiantly pursuing his arrant fleeing barks.

In the nearby field, the tail shook the bull

In bovine confusion at which horn to follow.

My skin abraded the day's eye.

The avenging breeze soaked me with sweat.

Water, hot land lusty, desired for me,

The harbor craved longingly for me.

The meandering fuming asphalt went down me

Through the flesh flotsam, to the quay.

I stripped the sea naked, it dived up me,

Outside, elusive sparrows swam...

Note: I have always had an acute need to wring my brain, so to speak. Up until now when I wake up in the mornings, I wake up a driven man and want nothing but to apply my mind to something difficult, to make something from nothing. Sometimes, I have no idea where I should start from or where I'm heading. I just have to produce something or be most uncomfortable.

HOW I LOOKED

With an old frond basket

I caught the clumsy thunder.

I sat and watched it blunder

About, seeking an exit.

Looking now in the mirror

I wondered how it sped before.

I swallowed the lightning

And kicked out the empty plate.

The poor curs were fighting

For it until it was too late.

Looking now in the mirror

I laughed at how I looked before.

I saw the foxy fox lost his tail,

Losing face before the tribe.

I watched his crafty scheming fail

To get the others his tales imbibe.

Looking how in the mirror

I laughed at how he looked before.

Landing in the speeding truck,

I caught them in a strange lock.

I took another leap and struck

My head on Macadam's rock.

Looking now in the mirror

I laughed at how I looked before.

All-day long and your benumbed flank

Trying to think out a book,

But ending with a sheet victoriously blank

That always a whole day took.

And looking after in the mirror

It was funny how I looked before.

Note: This was the result of wanting to write and not knowing what to write. As a teenager, I had a powerful desire to write but didn't know how to. There was no mentor, and I never found any book of instruction. I had no option than to either imitate the books that I enjoyed or invent my own way of writing. Many times I just sat from morning to evening scribbling in pencil on a blank foolscap sheet to see what comes out. I still have some of those sheets.

A GRADE II TEACHER'S

Oh! Those terrible urchins...

As if they watched to haunt one's sleep;

They shall taste of Mr Brown one day...

Busy crossing the highway.

From the class, along that path

To the pepper-soup joint. Maggie... cube...

Soup... Margaret... marry

Her one of these days... Her?

Cooks well... but bifocal denses... shit; lenses.

Big buttons... for pressing.

Nipples? No! Not again. No gain... pain?

Damn me. No. The crowing cock. Cock?

Not that. That new youth service girl. Mag.. must...

No; whore... see-through frock...

Fingering my... N. C. E.... hell certificate...

Stick my... chalk...

Innate... both sexes...

Hey! What's'at no...ise?

Shit! Idiot alarm clock...

I'm bloody... sorry.

Note: As a child, I was aware of the dangers that young bachelor teachers posed to the daughters of the host communities. This is my imagination of what goes through their minds when they happen to be at rest.

STRANGER

Stranger, stranger!

Won't you stay with us?

The road is rough

And the sun is set,

Pray, stay with us tonight

Kind sir, gentle ma,

I can't stay tonight.

The road is rough

And the sun is set,

But, considerate sire,

I love them so!

Traveler, traveler!

Please step in a while.

The bath is hot

And the bed is warm,

Please, sir,

Honor us tonight.

No, sir, no, ma,

I just can't. I just cannot.

Yes the bath is hot

And, no doubt, the bed is warm,

But I love the cold,

It's free.

But, sir,

My daughters can dance,

My niece sings well,

My wife cooks excellently,

My...

O Mister Hotelier,

Save your breath now,

Let me be on my way.

When the traveler becomes the sojourner

Maybe you might let us see your daughter!

Note: I don't even know why I wrote this safe that I was trying to amuse myself and rescue myself from a most boring day.

OCHUOLE

Ochuole, beautiful and wild,

There is something I crave of you;

It's buried like a pearl in your side;

Pluck it out for me, here is mine too.

Wild princess, o lovely queen,

The gilded path that leads to ruin,

Do you not recall the time

When we shunned all for fiery prime?

Now I can't sleep. I can't sleep.

I toss and turn every way

Vainly peering eyes trying to peep

Into the murkiness of the past that now holds sway.

The terrible restiveness,

The ghosts of long-gone warm nights,

Come upon me with heaviness

To wedge the lids of my sight.

Oh sweet and bitter are the juices

That I have sipped of fleeting youth.

Nightly they break their sluice

And flood me in my own broth.

Emerge from your carapace,

From behind a mask for a face;

It is the gleam and fragrance that draws,

Never the armor to all maws.

Now fly to me my succubus

My broiling body is burning.

Come part with me your enchanting kisses,

Your flaming, fabulous fondling.

Note: In his book, The Other Room, ... claimed that there never was a more lustful heart than that of a 15 years old boy.

THE LOST GENERATION

The treasured love of our fathers

Has succumbed to the will that inverts,

Has forever seeped beneath

Their parched overtrode soil

Like transient night-born mists

Upon the dried ever-thirsty deserts,

When the punctilious sun

Begins its daily toil.

The giver of the inheritance,

Knowingly or not, has it stolen

From the dazed, unlearned grip

Of our hope-jaded heirs.

Gone is the desired legacy,

The much-awaited direly won

By the rancor-split fathers:

Their sweat to the fires.

And since that accursed then,

Of options devoid we have daily dined

Upon the prickly, bonny proceeds

Of forced, cajoled or reasoned harlotry,

Welcomed night after night

Names bounties, and supped

Upon the poisoned profits

Wrenched from the Horn of Robbery.

So call us neither pimps nor thieves;

Desist from calumny,

Manna is gone with Moses, good friends.

Now is now, and not then,

For even by such galling exploits we barely subsist, hardly exist.

Why, we would have been long back

In the cyclical store of the elements.

So the ramparts of our faith

Collapsed. Hear it crash down

Splaying our bellies to fate's talons,

And to her armored grip, our necks.

The will, the vision, the hope,

Ballasts of our being, are all flown,

Emptied from our human husks,
Leaving mere hollow wrecks.

But we demand fair justice.
Let her prevail, but fortune? Never!
The Fair one may rip the reckless rag
That with false impartiality blinds her,
To confront her injudicious errors,
And carry them to the truth to repair,
But flagrant foolish Fortune
Is fervently blind... blind forever.

Have we not doggedly trod
Youth's know and sage-prescribed paths,
Straitened schooling, blinkered religion,
Torturing bells of physical regimen
But only some shaving if fate's lathe,
And only found more mouth-watering glimpses
Of more aspirations to slip away from?

Through fate's slimy slough
We have scrambled again and again.
We have trudged through fortunes' muck,
Nearly yielding the last breath to the mire.

Wearied is the worried flesh
Harried and dissipated in vain;
The valiant passenger-spirits
Bend their knees as they tire.

But we cannot just repose
To wither out, like a scathed weed. Why?
Though now towards blissful oblivion
The flesh is deliciously inclined,
Willing expiration is double defeat,
Which is to doubly die,
So, woefully supine on our back
We deny battle to assailants.

Dishonorable subjugation in battle
Is the lot of the unarmed in a struggle.
As the Sahara in a rainstorm,
So is acceptance defeat's defeat,
To clamp the mouth your lifeless mouth
Over the remnant of mettle
Than to be spilt into the mud
On your hope-of-reprieve vomit.

We will worm-eaten and rotten

In the palpability of our convictions

That the race was lost to us

By lacking the ways and means;

That, fairly, we would have compared with

If not outstripped and confounded

Our valiantly galloping juniors and peers

Swiftly vanishing into the distance.

But life's bloody battle

Is shorn of equal footing.

Fortune's lackeys, Time, Chance and Place,

Must be partial to one party.

By life's foul unfairness

I do not care to be seen

To set the feet, and race, of all

On equal line and parity.

Though let the winners be vindicated,

Let them revel in their justified song:

All plans fulfilled as arranged,

No essential fructification lost.

Be we know the maestro,

Conducive Chance prevailed so long

In its whim to have it composed,

And they believe the end their work.

It is our own quarry
Conspires against us.
Among the mutinous bunch,
Hope is the most traitorous one;
From expectation's zenith
Where it founded its lair,
It would raise you high and dash
You down, deeper than the last one.

Against if we have frittered away
That alchemists' old quarry, youthful vitality,
That horror whose birthright
Is to be born misfortune,
Tolling the galling half-truth
With infernal shuddering finality
That the desire may be anytime confronted
In a regretful moment inopportune.

Now was the holocaust to mate
With apocalypse and earth to ashes burn,
Hercules' lion-killing club
Could not force us to careless

For we were dismally desolate,

Infernally forlorn

While Hope rejoices

In its universal existence.

We thought with a beast's facilities,

Mistaking as a man should

Trespassing over the unmarked boundary

That he should not meddle with,

All in our quest of this odious rigor

Called life, which we call the Hopeless Cold

And pondered whether, for survival, we are fit

And if so, our niche in it.

When that mellifluous sense,

Our ancestors' matured tongue

That we luckily garnered from the spilling

Words of the exiled

Proves a weird, recondite practise,

A tongue most befuddling and strange,

From their prehistoric tombs

The custodians turned and smiled.

And even the foster tongue

Of our domicile of long

Of which we have been

But valiant learners

Soak no deeper

Than the span of the tongue

As it commonly is the lot

That befalls the homeless stranger.

Then the taunting savior,

Our dear Queen's English,

Like a wise but distant mother

Patiently enduring our coming along,

Lies somewhat shallower

Than we cared to wish for;

Gaudy, showy, hollow and brassy

As the tongue of a clamorous gong.

To gild our ancient falsehoods,

Imbue them with sheen seeming true,

We weave equivocal spells

Armed with malicious splayed tongues

And render the justifying story

Once and forever, old and new,

Accentuating the imprinted paths

That never was, for short of for long.

Yet we seek not trouble's respite

Not crave its abeyance.

Our knees have been battered aground

But we quake not before it.

We desire a little thing;

We merely crave weapons,

Instruments to heft and hew,

To deal our own blows with.

Inundate us like a waterfall fraught pebble

With a whole deluge of trouble

But with weapons too

With which to struggle and tackle

But we have none of faith at all;

It is fortune's gamble

To plump you into gods or devils.

Fate, gods, destiny and tomorrow,

All are obscure things,

All remote decider of events

That we would rather have palpably.

All are suspicious enemies

That oppose without being seen;

As for us, we would rather live,

Fight and die squarely.

Now the beggars are groveling

To the negated rhythm of their saying no,

Then let them never forget,

Let them stay their inquiring

About the new leavening

When it comes with the baked dough

Of which the wormwood

Has forbidden the eating.

And we spin the secret volition

Of thought not in words at all,

Isolated from the whole specie

By the thrashing throes of evolution

Our thoughts are mosaic images

In the mode of the craven animal,

We are the sequestered ones;

The lost generation.

Note: At a point, when I was about eighteen I felt that life was passing me by because it seemed to me that my latent ability was not being properly developed. At the same time, it seemed to me that my mates were going to university and I was at home doing nothing. I spent all my time reading big books, studying difficult things that had nothing to do with what I wanted to do with my life. I felt I was wasting.

ANOTHER LITTLE DEATH

Never the fiery orb shook itself awake

Or slipped down to where it slept

Over my emptiness unfilled with you,

Or my slumber or waking sleep you leave alone.

For long that adamantine redoubt that I endure for a heart

Thwarted Cupid's uncertain dart,

But now my blind bulwark has, vamoosed,

Before your impartial eyes,

Disrobing my icy vaunt for its crawling lies.

And I'm drunk with you:

My love for you has gone to my head

Setting my besotted spirit ablaze with your ravaging flame

And entice me with, instead of one of you,

A haunting myriad; Yet I love all of you.

My enchantress, I'm ensnared by the spell of your charm

And entangling the more each mournful mocking chime

But change it not; I'll rather be reminded

It's to the end of time.

Time is my love and my love is but time;

It ever endures like the crouching mountains

As after desire's death, it will still remain

But you are blind, deaf and mute, and must rear me on pain.

Now, what am I to you but an incommoding bore?

My face burns as from wasps from the slamming of your door.

Is it because they utterly outrank me, your scented and suitors well-named

Bearing appellations that would barely sweeten yours?

Refrain from asking my station in life or name,

Or whatever vague home where I was nurtured;

Neither have I been introduced to your acquaintance, fame,

Nor hope to be soon, and loathe my title judged.

Sorrow, oh sorrow. I'm shorn of the gracious name,

And I don't have the required symbol, the people's qualifying means

Though truly and equally I rage with the Cold Flame

Further from the forbidding people my flame flickers and leans.

Now you're steeped in truculence; at last, again, you're angry,

For you couldn't care less. Your usually dainty step,

Because in and out you're thoroughly mad at me,

Seems not to be airily sprung with an over-measure of pep.

Your steps that invariably seem to my eager ears never waxing,

But like an over-wary sparrow, always flitting away

As the treacherous floor betrays me (it's made for betraying),

But we must commune so why don't you stay?

By the very honeyed words the man was falsely cajoled,

By your ancestor, through which your race tongue-slay,

By your given garrulousness by which my kind was deceived,

I desire your auspicious audience; by it all, stay!

Ah! Hear; my love supersedes all your good names;

They dim and wane and must fade away with time.

They are consumed to oblivion in its lusty, devouring flames

But my love will soar, rising, the phoenix in their fires.

You're the blazing fire and my love for you the faggot;

Pile it high, lick around it, overwhelm and engulf it;

The master's hand is free with the bondservant's lot.

Oh yes, it will burn me but won't love be lit!

So love me, love me, my haughty beautiful one,

Love me now; love me while we're yet strangers,

My sad visage has never turned anyone into stone.

Even one daring glance, I beg of you, without your fears.

Then let me be the lowly earth and you the distant skies,

I am matt and muddy, you studded with stars.

Let my natural distance and your cosmic aloofness shatter the lies

That our meeting is forbidden, us being utterly dissimilar.

Good. If you hate the near then glance at the horizon.

Look and consider; no two ever further apart

But, there, out of scrutiny's prison, they meet and become one:

Is it not ironic by a sweet trick of the distance that they beat with one heart?

O to die by love! All of a sudden to puff out!

Dull, unlovely, foul it is to gutter, pine and slowly waste.

Oh, to cease to exist at once, in the wee span of a shout

Like an unwitting phantom surprised, in multiplied haste.

Yeah, an instantaneous love-death if the one for the craver;

Sweetly appropriate, justifiable to the end,

The lone counting avenger against the disdainful slayer

That once guffawed at the pieces of the loyal heart she rent.

Then to victoriously split open the jeering eye from the grave

The sweetest wee bit split of a crack created ever

And peep at the former slave now turned into a collared slave,

And I gone, forever gone beyond beck and call, the enslaver!

I would leer leisurely from the putrescent grave

At the cupped tear-filled flower and spit at the disgusting tribute

Slewing in her very essence, siphoning of her vase of life;

Leaving her a spectral leftover; an exfoliating ghost lover...

No! No! Death is love's blasphemy; the reaper will come soon enough,

Obsessive, single-minded, non-rebuttable, it must come to stay,

And it will come anytime, but now only now is love

Now the feeling is flesh and now is its way.

I would have created that looming mountain mansion

That infinitely infests the salubriousness of my waking dream

Then I would say, "Let there be flowers and blooming passion."

And to water them by, "be!" a merry gurgling stream.

I would have cried in a Voice, "Let there be silence!"
For the sound of love is from and for but two,
Alone within the mountains save nature's uplifting noise
Would I have to hear? O, and music thrilling and true.

But for the righteous forbidder, dull, dull reality,
Ruthless enemy of unfettered beauty,
O that world-panorama flips to my fancy
Would I possess my love although she not me!

I would steal it to the people's priggish frown
And snatch if from her hewn hands and declare it ours,
Not for them, that vague them, but for her
And that stolen, it's delicious, but remembered, it sours.

Then I must be on tenterhooks upon my love's veiled consent
And must divine the eagerness beneath the veneer of negation,
My purse must purchase the equally share present
As if ever the mutual sprang from a volition.

So, invade, the stiff tail of this charging millennia
And flee the hungry head of the impatient another,
I shall be left in this lurch by your primal essence;

Your everlasting adorer and lover.

Note: Ensconced deep within the forests on the outskirts of Ibadan, where I had no chance of ever meeting the fairer sex, I still found myself tortured by the things of the heart. The surprising thing was that the turgidity that filled me was directed to no one.

OF MALABRESSES, 1996

As I trudged down Nudist highway

I jotted as my muse began to sing.

She sang of how it's okay

For them to display.

You need not stoop

To glimpse enough to whoop.

They forget that the sweetest of all joy

Quickly fills then begins to cloy...

That's if a poor boy escaped the mesmerism

Of staring into the yawning chasm

Of stainless thighs and white panties

Until an okada and he intersected in a final point

Of twisted metals and broken bones.

Note: Some years later, in 1995, I gained admission to the University of Calabar to study political sciences. As of then, there were motorcycle taxis plying all nooks and crannies of the campus. It was not uncommon for the young short-skirted girls to board a bike to class. But it was not a common sight to me to see girls sitting with an apparent lofty disregard for modesty.

TO MY AFRO

You of the Clippers,

Before you devastate this jungle-like verdure,

The nurtured foliage of my ebony fields,

Do you know Afro?

It is perched upon the midnight brow

To guard the beauties as they grow.

Pluck it from the wild of the jungle,

Cut and carve if from this dread tangle;

It is a calabash black and velvety

Crowning the black and his beauty.

Note: I wore an Afro hairstyle for most of the latter part of my teenage years; it was my message to the world that I was a different person and that I could do whatever I wanted. It was also a sign to myself of my intellectualism, which I then called "Freemanism". For years I ignored my father's plea to cut it as Afros were no longer in style even then. I only cut it after dropping out of the university to join the army, and only because it was a requirement for enlistment.

A NAMELESS WARRIOR

I'm a nameless warrior,

I fight a nameless battle.

I hide my face in my body,

Manliness in womanhood,

Pains in calluses,

Even my vaunted bravery

I veil in my cowardice,

For when I meet my master

I congratulate him

For a good job

Of stomping into the mud my testicles.

I'm no longer afraid to stare into my wound

That I may fully feel the total redemption.

Yesterday was section battle drills.

I learnt new tactics to use

That the same irritable battle

Could be won in two different ways;

To charge and kill, or be killed,

Or to surrender and kill, or be killed.

Note: There is a need to obliterate your other-self in order to be a good soldier. At the recruitment depot of the Nigerian army, instructors call it "civilian mentality". It is a disease from which the army saves a recruit. If necessary, the Drill Sergeant curses or flogs it out of him. The wise soldier submerges his real self so that he can blend, yet find an oblique way of realizing his individuality in a system that is built upon the standardization of personalities.

WINNING IN LOSS

I tried to sneak up on life

By living as if I'm not,

Thinking that, by pure subterfuge,

Creeping in through the back roads,

I might enter through the back doors

Into the front stage of unannounced success.

On the night of the séance

I immolated myself to our gods.

But the smoke from my soul rose

Beneath their averted heads

To smear their sneering beards.

Left alone, I found the strength of a man;

He could be anything he chooses,

Bear any of a multitude of names,

Touching, feeling, smelling

His innermost desire.

Now, I no longer take flight,

Losing myself in the maze of life.

I chop my mountains into convenient stairs

For I know not the strength of man,

And tremble in awe of it.

Note: Life began to look like a battle to me, and I became aware that I was entirely on my own when the chips were down. Victorious warfare relies on psychological and even physical subterfuges, so I began to carry over strategies and tactics learnt in the army into my personal life.

NEW YAM FESTIVAL

I miss again the annual festival,

The careful planning,

The exact execution,

The bittersweet honing of knives

And spurting and spurting of hot blood

Into the ever-thirsty ancestral ground.

I'm always hundreds of miles away

Estranged from our re-birthing tradition

By chance, thoughts, and alliance,

But the gall of the sacrificial beast

Passes to me after the ceremony.

Making a living has made me a blasphemer

Living to desecrate the old ways and the elders;

I'm now my own acolyte.

You many go on offering sacrifices,

But always do pass me the gall, please?

Note: The New Yam festival marks the beginning of the yam harvest season. It is a time of celebrating the end of the old season and the beginning of a new one, so it represents a local New Year celebration that for us surpasses the Western New Year. Sons of the soil from everywhere chose this occasion to come together and renew their fraternal and ethnic bonds. For the seventeen years that I spent in the army, I was unable to attend this traditional annual re-birthing.

NIGHTGUARD, OJO CANTONMENT, 2002

The officer:

Guard! Guard! Guard!

You're mad! You're mad!

Why do you let this man harass me?

Did you come here to sleep?

Arrest this man at once!

The man:

I'm a soldier like you,

I'm not a criminal.

Let me explain myself.

The judgment:

Okay, soldiers, let him go.

The next morning:

Guards! You are all still sleeping!

Wake up now!

Come for your morning tea.

Push that truck until it starts!

The reward:

Thank you. Bye.

I have no "welfare" for you.

Note: Serving in the military can sometimes be cold and cruel. This poem fixes in my mind forever the unfeeling and wilful wickedness that some officers hide beneath the guise of being soldierly. The words were taken from an actual event.

NIGHT SENTRY

The good things are with me,

I'm not afraid.

Though the night be pitch-suffused

And the never-familiar Night Sounds,

Each infinite in its sneaky, jarring round,

Their unnameable, unseen, emasculating melodies

Cloying the night's awful sweetness

With their permeating primordial divisions

Wafting among the Eternal presences,

From which I choose the Good ones;

They are with me,

And I'm not afraid.

Note: The most important military missions are carried out in the period between sunset and dawn because the darkness is the great equalizer, the element in which every soldier should revel. But, first, he must privately come to terms with the evil that lurks in the dark.

A CONDOLENCE VISIT

Once again a flash of fated chance
Struck through our one aging armor,
Piercing through our scarred bones
To sear our collective marrow.

I dread the moment of condolence
In futile hope that this cup is not ours
But, like a portion of a spent nightmare,
Designed to fade and then pass away.

But it does not. It seems it is here to stay;
I have seen it hobbling impossibly real
Down the cement of the cold passage,
Trying hard not to seem invalid.

I wish to rejoice in your acceptance,
Your denying the face its normal grimaces,
But dreams of braced bones falsely knitting
Snatched it all away from me.

Yet you need not put up a front for me

For I am here to feel your pain with you,

Take it all away if only I could;

But you contain it, and I marvel.

So, should we now be grateful

For a spared but disabled life,

Or maybe envy the lucky dead

Who now knows nor feels no pain?

Note: I went to visit a relative who had just survived a car accident in which most of the passengers died.

GIRLFRIEND

"What a beautiful girl you are,"
I told your friend a while ago
In cunning hope she'll deliver
The message I could not.

Then, inflating my pricked courage,
I stammered out the rehearsed litany,
While our friends were very busy,
One reading, the other cooking…

But how come they strangely shook their heads
As you first refused my advances,
Or nodded in synchronization
When you, at last, said "yes"?

I began to tremble at the possibility
That my prayers might just be answered
With you, delivered to me,
A heaven-sent chicken to a hawk.

Having sent a sister on a wild goose chase

I laid a tremble-handed table

But you were raptured before Easter,

Timely snatched away from my talons.

You are not my desire's embodiment

Or my motive might have been wrong.

Now, would there be more than meets the eyes

And of transgression purges my purpose?

Your trite love declarations now lay before me

Burning holes in the sincerity of my purpose.

So, should I now leap in faith alone

Or in cold machine-like calculation?

BREAKING WIND

All the meals of these past three days

Couldn't add up to one full meal.

By a natural miracle

I digested all completely,

The fibers too turned to nutrients…

But three days was a day too long

Without the needed downloading.

So, practicing self-suggestion,

I modulated my breathing,

Downed five liters of water,

Immersed in a vast detachment,

I visualized lucky outcomes.

Then, my Richter scale pricked up

To sense the tiniest seismic guts stirring

Tickling my retired entrails.

Overjoyed at this benevolence

I sprinted to my starved toilet

To perch like a child awaiting

The gift from its mother's journey.

But almost an hour later,

Though stale air managed to escape,

Things remained roughly the same.

Note: Even as a soldier, I still found that the old irregularity of eating had still caught up with me. This time due to the nature of military duties. Sometimes we were deployed on guard duties on which it was impossible to cook or buy food, even though the army was not supplying any kind of food.

FROM CONFERENCE AT EL GENEINA

I made a promise to my sister

When I called her from El-Geneina

That, soon, on disembarkation day,

We shall meet again at Calabar.

But fate taught me a bitter lesson

About promises, winds and aircraft

When our chopper was just swallowed up,

Jonah in the belly of a sandstorm.

Then I lost sight of my dear sweet earth;

For three hours, we only bumbled around,

Circling round and round like a blind bat.

Though I tried not to worry at all

For I can't change a black hair to white,

Yet I couldn't cut the looped movie

Or burning twisted metal and flesh.

My life didn't flash before my eyes

But the thought of what I'd now miss;

The fine babes, fine music and fine food

That will now forever be wasted.

Note: The officer commanding the protection force flew to El-Geneina for a conference. I, being his orderly, escorted him there. Four days later, as we were flying back to Foro Baranga, the location of our own Military Group Site, our helicopter ran into a sandstorm. I remember one female Ghanaian police inspector asking the pilot, "how far to El Fashir?" The pilot looked ominously at us and answered, "Just pray." But I did not pray.

MISSING IN ACTION

When the rivers of your souls
Flowed to the Niger Delta,
Your thoughts were on your Duties
And the usual RCA.

You performed Malu's magic
To exorcize Taylor's demons,
Sparing us from the just terror
Of his peacekeeping on us.

You did not in your hearts know
That the night that you banished
With your blood in Liberia
Might fall in your hometown.

My friend from Bayelsa
Told me of the burials,
The weeping on the NTA
Of families mourning deaths.

My friend from Bayelsa
Now pray for a new Odi
Forgetting that some time ago,
He boasted of ancient rites...

The sharpness of cutlasses
Fell like the broadsides on his back,
The iron spikes bent backwards,
Against his stomach, a reed.

They walked a deadly gauntlet,
Egbesu dance under the moon,
Promising the deflection
Of all 7.62 balls...

Somebody promised that khaki
Was immune from all sorcery.
But now, we know much better
From the mouths of the corpses.

Note: As a child, I was told that soldiers would kill their mothers even their mothers when ordered to do so. This might be laying it on too thick, but in a certain sense, the only loyalty a soldier has is for his colleagues and the Army, despite the conflict of interests that surrounds the deaths when they operate in their own towns and villages. Egbesu is the god of just of the NIger Delta people, who make up a significant number of the military forces operating against militants in the creeks, who believe the deity could protect them from bullets.

NIGHT SENTRY, IDON

I sit in the cold before a roaring fire,

Staring into its blinding glare

Regardless of its nullifying my sight,

Its mocking the futility

Of my listening for the invisible footstep,

Battling with the sweet lie

Of one post by day, two posts by night,

As Morpheus tied his black blindfold

Over the eyes of the second post,

A lone pair of eyes

Watching out for fellow warriors.

Within the safety of a wood fire before my,

Tow diesel lamps to my left and right,

A blanket of billions of stars above

And all ensconced in the black night,

I face, across the razor wire,

The inscrutable black shadows of the night savannah,

Aware of invisible watching eyes

Awaiting opportunity to strike.

What if we have just one enemy

That moves with the feet of an adept?

What if our enemy

Has given us the leaf of sleep?

What if my relentless scanning of dark edges

Saved us from all messy deaths

Except for the elite efficiency of the invisible man?

So I gave the fire my back.

While the lava of my buttocks

Melted by the furnace behind me

Trickled down behind my legs,

Now, the phallus continues to remain,

Immensely torn between two worlds,

The frozen tip of an iceberg.

Above, the impudent stars wink their Morse to me,

My awareness spread out like tanks

Dug to catch rain Saharan rain,

I tried to decode their cryptic message.

As I listened unheedingly to their age-old wisdom

Shed some light on my martial fate,

The silhouette of knowledge

Fell on my consciousness

That the only wisdom on earth for me

Is the awareness that

I'm entirely on my own.

Note: This deals with thoughts that flick through my mind as I struggled to stay awake to keep watch in the night while the other soldiers slept.

SECOND TARGET

When I was a civilian

We shot at a round target.

We become heroes

By hitting the bull's eye,

That innermost circle,

That nothing of nothing

That we shot at, hoping

It wouldn't ever bleed.

Then, it seemed just a play,

This range classification,

As if far is the day

That we'll face flesh and blood.

But one night, like a bad joke

I found myself drawing the bead,

Tracking my fellow man

With the muzzle of my AK.

What am I doing here,

A snake crawling in the mud,

Beaten by a drizzle in some strange Savannah,

Mindful of an untimely shot?

I prayed not to squeeze the trigger

As he came within point-blank range,

But with the other corner of my mouth

I prayed he wouldn't escape from me.

Note: *The first prospect of taking a human life in the line of duty and the requirement of not proving to be a coward in combat, as well as the balancing of one's superstitious and religious beliefs with the exigencies of the military profession poses a dilemma that one has to resolve alone.*

THE WARRIOR'S SHAME

Shame on the warrior who, when he awakes

Can't lift up the earth a hundred times.

Does he think this my father's job

Was created for his amusement

That he ignored to build his strength?

Shame on the warrior when at all jests

Rather than wear his war face,

Who takes his mock battles as a play,

Know him not that his present sweating

Is to lessen his battlefront bleeding?

Shame on the warrior who forgets the reason

For which he fled his father's home.

Was it not that before manhood

He may achieve a confirmed kill?

You deny now in peacetime your love of war.

Shame on the warrior who flinches
While aiming at a man-shaped target.
So you think it is a stage show,
Something you act, and then forget,
Never hoping to face flesh and blood?

Shame on the warrior who hesitates
To pull the bayonet or the trigger
In some concrete warren or steamy jungle
And deal the perfect death in a prescribed form.
He shall earn a medal for his comrades' death.

Shame on the warrior, who lived by the gun,
Who as a child dreamt of bloody victories,
Becoming the toast of grizzled warriors
But when his time came surely
Refused to lay by his rifle, and quietly die.

Note: Many do not realize that soldiering is like a religion. Some have likened it to a secret society. There can be no such thing as a half-hearted soldier. A soldier who realizes that he is actually a warrior, and is not in the job only for the salary, knows that, as they say, "the business of war is killing". He would do all that is necessary to himself in the best possible shape to perform his primary functions, or else he would become the means of performing the primary functions of an enemy soldier.

FIRST HIV TEST

At last, the bitter-sweet wind of fate
Blew me to that horrible junction
Where the bisectors of fate shared me
Into parts of an objective test.

I ride to Shendam town to a lab
To disprove an old suspicion
That these pimples, these lesions and fevers
Couldn't be anything but that thing.

I watch in trepidation my blood
Sucked into your translucent syringe.
Though I smiled and bantered light-heartedly,
I chanted the mantra of psalm sixteen…

But strange is the reversal I suffered,
My relief after my donation;
Knowing my fate has fled my hands,
I went in search of a good restaurant.

Note: Since the year 2002 I had lived with the horror of the possibility of being HIV positive. Any abnormality I noticed on my body was a sure symptom. I got to the point that, after suffering a series of serious malaria bouts, I assumed that I had already gotten it so there was no longer any need to protect myself. Yet I was afraid of going for a test until I was forced to take it by the army as part of the medical checkups for participating in the African Union Mission in Sudan (AMIS).

ARMY BLUES

Should you be ordered to sit on your head
Right before your youth corper girlfriend
For thirty minutes till you see and smell red,
Take heart, bros, for there is a name for it.

Should you perform five days' extra duty
For watching TV on muster parade,
Duty has never killed anyone.
Endure, bros, there is a name for it.

Should, after patrolling Janjaweed land,
Your AK won't cock no matter what,
Don't be surprised, for you aren't the first.
Stand at ease, for there is a name for it.

Should some of these strange events
That sweetens up the rugged life befall you,
Don't take them too much to your only heart
For they are all called funny-funny things.

Note: This deals with the inescapable discrepancies between the military and civilian lives, which the soldier has to stomach. The inconsistencies that are quite normal, and are what mark out the soldier that would obey when given the order; they advance as if it were the most ordinary thing in the world to walk or run into the flight of bullets. At last these events are taken by the soldier as nothing but one more reason to express amusement.

PADRE'S HOUR IN FORO BARANGA, 2007

Let us not boast

Of power, knowledge and wisdom,

But only boast

Of just our love in the Lord:

Yet my AK

Sleeps quietly between my legs.

What will I do

When brothers Janjaweed charge at our camp

During worship,

My fully loaded magazines

Near my AK?

The holy war

That will spew from this tent

Might engulf us

From both sides of the razor wire.

Then, in Heaven,

Who might we judge was right or wrong?

Note: This deals with the ambiguity of being a Christian as well as a soldier. I believed that one can be either at any time but not both at the same time. A soldier is a warrior. If one should think of the qualities of a good warrior, the least of which is an affinity for violence and a lack of fear of killing, one would find that they are the opposite of core Christian values. As a soldier, I always get a deep feeling of hypocrisy whenever I enter a church. I would like to be a good Christian, but that should be after the army has discharged me from service.

SHOPPING IN FORO BARANGA MARKET

I never knew I'll meet someone like you

In a Godforsaken North African market.

Although, from the excruciating pain,

Born of a sudden blossoming of blood,

That hit my heart like a sniper's bullet,

I know I'll never see you again.

When my eyes mistakenly met your eyes

I was afraid to look straight at you

That I may not flout your theocracy.

So, hidden beneath my combat helmet

And AHQ's recommended dark glasses,

I beamed the ghost of a smile at you.

When you smiled back from behind your parted veil

And your mother, resembling you, smiled too,

I knew my dowry would be taken...

But you lifted your stuff and walked away.

You didn't look back, but you won't forget me.

In my country, I too will remember you.

Note: I was shocked to find myself in a situation that might have been called love at first sight in a different setting. We obey national and military laws that forbid undue socializing, but there is no law capable of fettering the heart from its natural inclinations.

KADUNA

Faraway in some Special Forces sangar,

Steamy jungle or desert oven,

I'm surprised to catch myself

Filled with thoughts of you.

The long spokes of your ancient rays

Seek out my heart to skewer.

Despite your many schisms,

Your countless little pogroms

That now and then defiled our peace,

Denouncing you to me as a place

To sow the seeds of my life and wealth,

And sink my final taproot,

My heart's needle still points to the North.

I took you for a small muddy stream

Swarming with worms and algae,

Infested with predatory crocodiles.

But hooked out, I flip about,

A fish beached upon foreign soils

Till I'm able to dive back into your muddy waters.

Note: Kaduna is the name of the town in northern Nigeria. It is the location of my regiment where I served for almost two decades. Kaduna town is named after the River Kaduna, which means "crocodiles". The town never looked like a town to miss to me until when I found myself far away on guard duties, patrols or international missions.

FROM NIGERIAN WITH LOVE

Years ago I escaped the poisonous fangs

That pierced into my shell

Thinking to cocoon myself in the comradeship

Of men fighting to work out

The sick algebra complicating our lives.

Suddenly, a fleshy meteorite

Breaking to a stop,

I found myself at Nyala,

Biting dust in sandy Sudan.

Blown by the winds of destiny,

Borne by the butterfly of destiny,

I opened my weary eyes,

A puzzled sacrificial lamb

In the dusty oven of Foro Baranga.

A decade ago, I prayed to God

That the rudder of my destiny

Be placed firmly in my grasp,

That I may be the discoverer

Of how the loveless could squeeze out love

To glue back a warring nation…

Now, at the festivity for which I prayed,

I began to pray again.

Note: The individual is powerless when he is caught up in the intricate machinery of the army as it kicks into action. Life in the military is one of sacrifice in which one overlooks one's individual will and identity. One becomes, no matter one's uniqueness, only that which the army allowed one to be.

ABOUT THE AUTHOR

Odey Richard Odey

Richard Odey enjoys reading and writing thrillers, science fiction, fantasy, and African literary fiction. Currently working on his novel, The Juju Man, he lives in Nigeria with his wife and two sons.

NOTES